# GERMS!

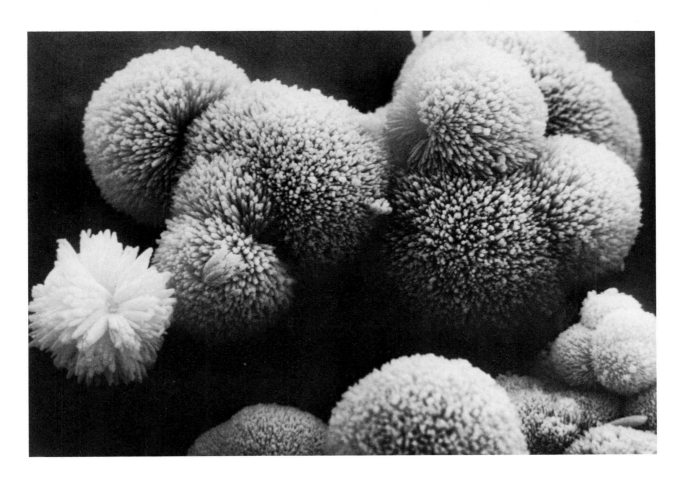

**Dorothy Hinshaw Patent**

HOLIDAY HOUSE / NEW YORK

To germ-fighting scientists, doctors, and nurses everywhere

I wish to thank my father, H. Corwin Hinshaw, M.D.,
my husband, Greg, and my sons, David and Jason,
for their help with this book.

Library of Congress Cataloging in Publication Data

Patent, Dorothy Hinshaw.
  Germs!

  Includes index.
  Summary: Explains what germs are, how they attack
the body, and how the body protects itself against
their onslaught. Includes material on immunization
and research in disease control.
  1. Communicable diseases—Juvenile literature.
2. Immunity—Juvenile literature.  [1. Communicable
diseases.  2. Immunity]  I. Title.
RC113.P37  1983      616'.01      82-48749
ISBN 0-8234-0481-1

*The photo on the title page
shows crystals of a new germ-
fighting medicine called
Azactam.* E. R. SQUIBB & SONS,
INC.

# Contents

WHAT IS A GERM?                                        5

DISCOVERING GERMS                                     11

GETTING WELL                                          14

GETTING A SHOT                                        18

ANTIBIOTICS                                           22

HOW GERMS MAKE US SICK                                29

THE FUTURE                                            36

INDEX                                                 40

*All of the round blobs in this electron microscope photo
are bacteria which cause tooth decay. (Magnified
approximately 30,000 times.)* COURTESY OF THE PROCTER &
GAMBLE COMPANY

# What Is a Germ?

What makes people get sick? For a long time, no one knew. Some people thought a cool breeze could give them head colds, or that "bad air" caused a serious disease. As long as the causes of sickness were unknown, it was hard to help sick people. But now we know that germs bring about many illnesses. Germs are so small that we can't see them with our eyes.

There is a whole world of tiny living things that can be seen only with a microscope. A microscope has lenses which can make things look thousands of times their real size. Before there were microscopes, scientists didn't know about invisible life forms such as germs. But now we know a great deal about them.

Scientists call such tiny living things "microorganisms." Microorganisms are everywhere. A tiny square of your skin can contain 100,000 of them. There are more microorganisms on one human body than there are humans on the entire Earth!

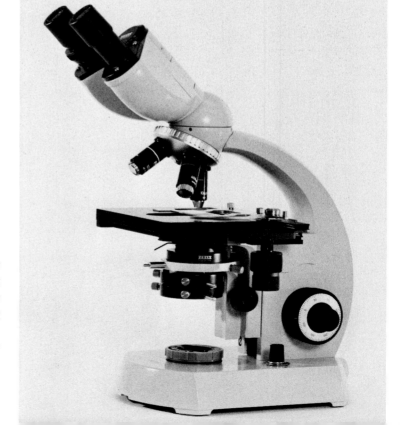

*This is a light microscope. It uses light rays which pass through lenses to make things look bigger than they really are. A light microscope can make things appear over 1,000 times as big as their real size.* COURTESY CARL ZEISS, INC., THORNWOOD, NY

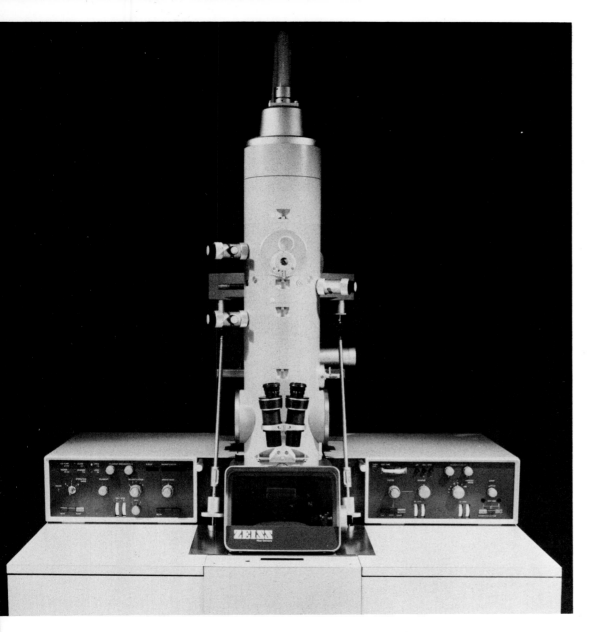

*This big machine is an electron microscope. It can make things look more than 100,000 times as big as they really are.*
COURTESY CARL ZEISS, INC., THORNWOOD, NY

7

Most microorganisms are harmless. But there are also some that are troublemakers, or germs.

Many germs are types of bacteria. Bacteria are very small microorganisms that live just about everywhere. With a regular light microscope, bacteria look like tiny dots, rods, or commas. Most bacteria cannot hurt us. But some can make people sick. Tuberculosis, diphtheria, food poisoning, strep throat, and many other diseases are caused by bacteria.

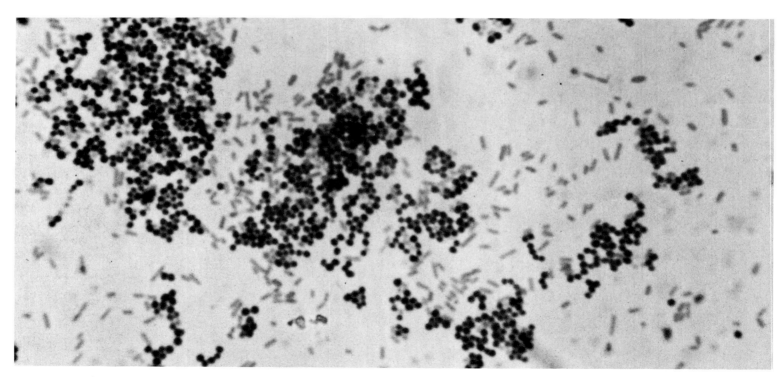

*There are two different kinds of bacteria in this picture. The dark dots are called "staph" (Staphylococcus aureus) and cause several kinds of sickness. The oblong shapes are called "E. coli" (Escherichia coli). They live in the human intestine.*
DR. LEON J. LEBEAU, DEPT. OF PATH., U. OF ILL. MED. CENTER

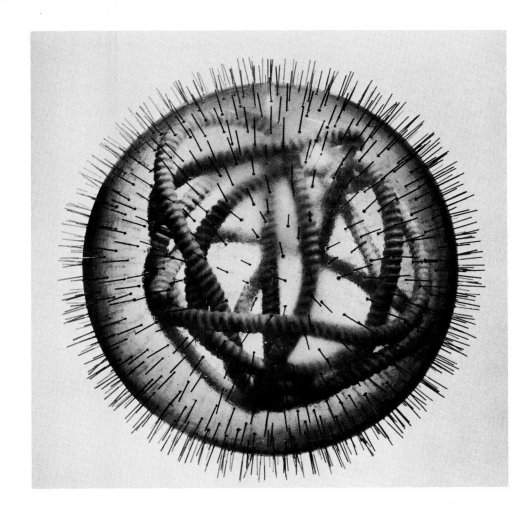

*This is a giant plastic model of a measles virus.* PFIZER INC.

The smallest germs are called "viruses." Viruses cause head colds and the flu as well as other illnesses.

Not all germs are bacteria or viruses. Some are bigger and have different shapes. Malaria and African sleeping sickness are caused by such bigger germs.

The germs which make you sick need to live inside your body in order to multiply. The "sickness" you feel is the result of the germs growing and multiplying in your body.

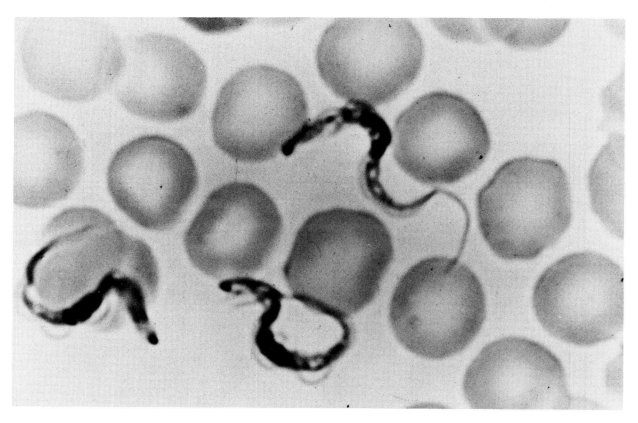

*The wavy objects in this photo are germs which cause African sleeping sickness. They live in the blood. The round shapes are red blood cells.* PHOTOGRAPH BY CAROLINA BIOLOGICAL SUPPLY COMPANY

# Discovering Germs

Before 1876, the causes of most diseases were unknown. There were few medicines which helped people get well. But in that year, a great discovery was made. A German doctor named Robert Koch proved that bacteria could cause a disease called "anthrax." The French scientist, Louis Pasteur, also uncovered important facts about bacteria during the 1800s. Once people knew that bacteria could make them sick, scientists discovered the germs that caused many serious bacterial sicknesses—and in only twenty-five years! Ways of preventing a number of these diseases were also developed.

As they studied diseases, these scientists were surprised to find that many were not caused by bacteria. One way of finding the dangerous bacteria was to push fluids containing the germs through a filter with holes so tiny that bacteria could not pass through them. If the liquid which came through the filter no longer caused sickness, that meant the germs were caught by the filter. They were bacteria or bigger germs. But some filtered fluids could still cause sickness. They contained viruses, the tiniest germs. Because they are so small, viruses are hard to study. It took a long time before scientists were able to learn much about them.

*Each dot in this photo is a polio virus. Polio used to be a feared childhood disease. It can destroy muscles and even kill. (Magnified approximately 180,000 times.)* MARCH OF DIMES

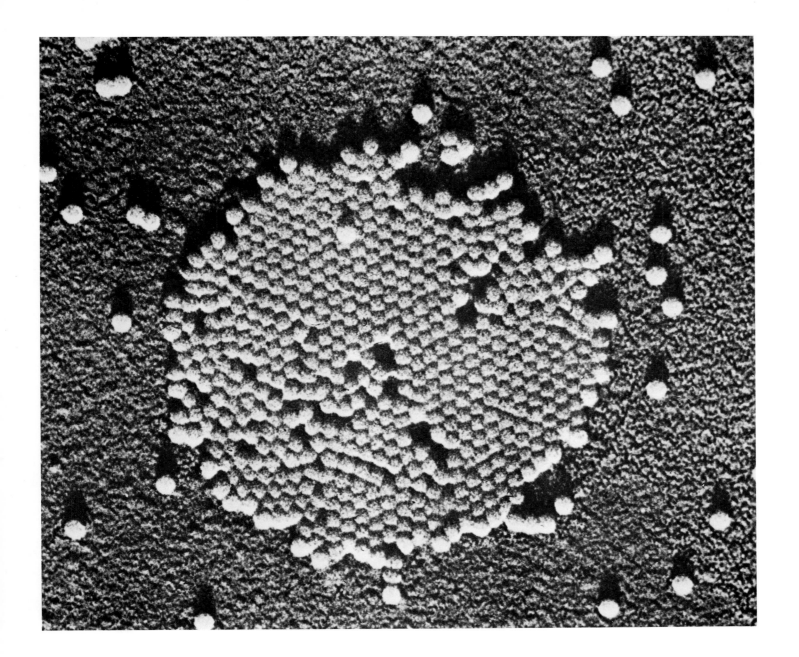

# Getting Well

Your body has good ways of fighting off germs. When germs get inside your body, it can tell that they don't belong. Special cells in the blood called "macrophages" (this means "big eaters" in the Greek language) attack the germs, surround them, and digest them.

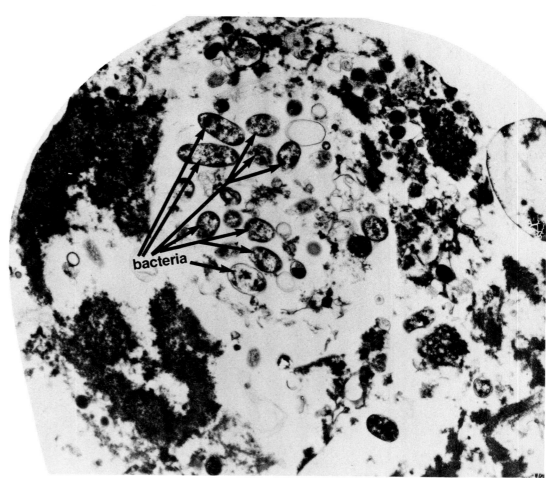

*Here is a photo showing Legionnaire's Disease bacteria inside a macrophage.*
CENTERS FOR DISEASE CONTROL, ATLANTA, GA.

bacteria

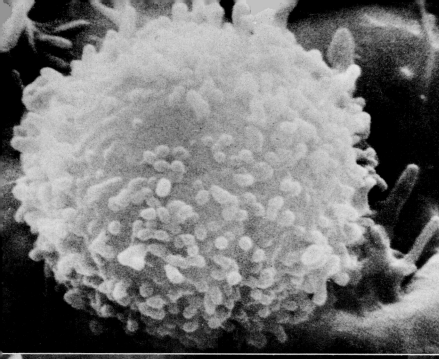

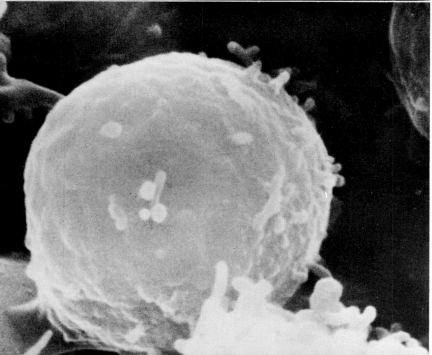

Other cells make chemicals called "anti-bodies," which can attach to the outside of the germs. The antibodies work along with germ fighters called "T cells" to kill germs. Chemicals in the blood also help fight germs. One of these is called "interferon."

*The top photo shows an antibody-producing cell.*

*The photo on the left shows a T cell. It works with antibodies to kill germs. Both of these photos were taken with an electron microscope.* MEMORIAL SLOAN-KETTERING CANCER CENTER AND ROCKEFELLER UNIVERSITY

15

Each kind of germ has an outer layer that's different from the outer layer of other kinds of germs. For example, the outer layer of the tuberculosis germ is not the same as the outer layer of the diphtheria germ. Antibodies which can attach to tuberculosis germs can't fasten onto diphtheria germs. So the body must make different antibodies to fight different germs. Before enough antibodies of a new kind can be made, cells which can make them have to grow and multiply. This process takes time. While your body is building up this antibody machinery, you are feeling sick. But when lots of the right antibodies are being turned out, you can fight off the germs and get well.

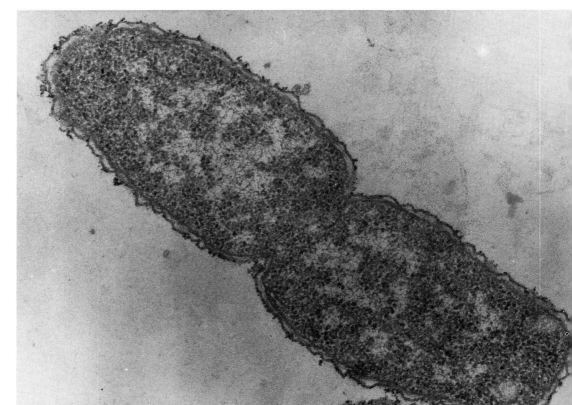

*These bacteria are about 60,000 times their real size. You can see the outer layer on the cells.*
NATIONAL INSTITUTES OF HEALTH,
NATIONAL INSTITUTE OF ALLERGY
AND INFECTIOUS DISEASES

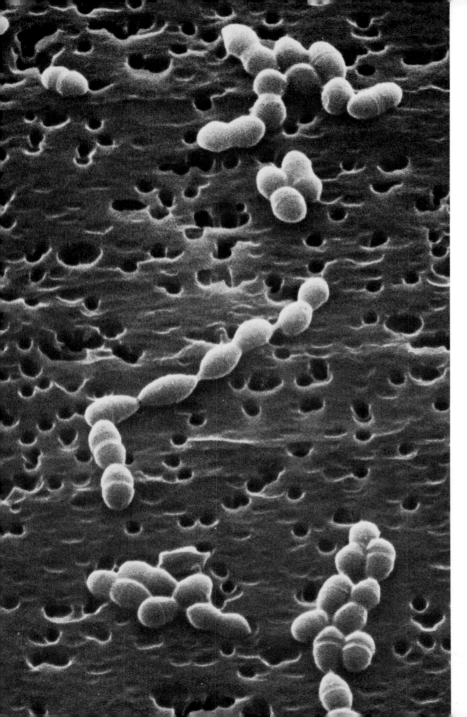

Once your body has been attacked by a particular germ, the antibody-making cells that overcome it remain in your body. They are ready to go into action if that same germ comes along again. So the same kind of germ can rarely make you sick more than once.

Why, then, do people get head colds often in their lives and catch the flu over and over? It turns out that many different viruses can cause a cold or the flu. But after you have had a certain cold germ, that one probably won't affect you again.

*These are strep bacteria* (Streptococcus). *They can cause strep throat, scarlet fever, and rheumatic fever. The holes are spaces in the material underneath the bacteria. (Magnified approximately 10,000 times.)* COURTESY OF ELI LILLY AND COMPANY

# Getting a Shot

There are some diseases you will never have because you are "immunized," or protected, against them. Most children today are given a DPT shot to keep them from getting diphtheria, whooping cough (called "pertussis"), and tetanus. They are also immunized against polio with a squirt into the mouth instead of a shot. These diseases are very serious and can kill people. Many children get immunized against measles, mumps, and rubella, too.

*The tiny circles in this photo are rubella viruses.* CENTERS FOR DISEASE CONTROL, ATLANTA, GA.

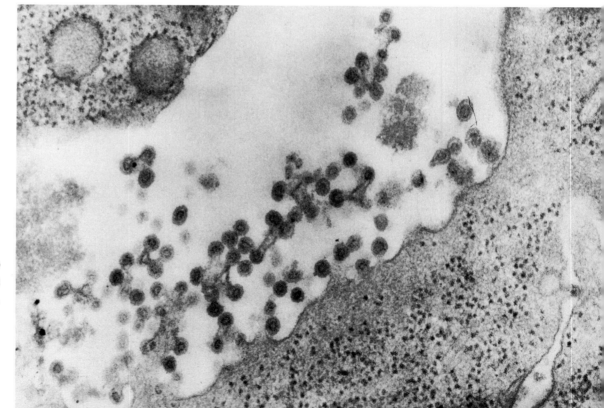

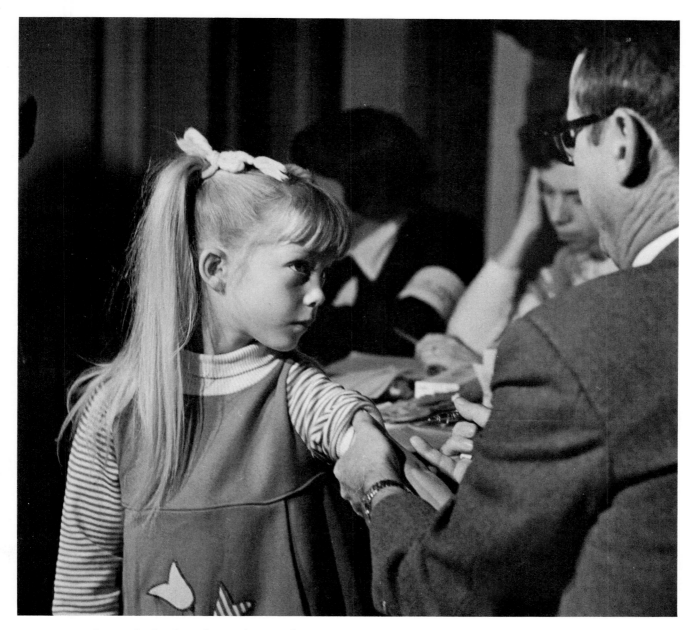

*Shots may hurt a little, but that is better than getting sick.*
*This girl is being immunized against rubella.* MARCH OF DIMES

How can a shot protect you from sickness? When you get a shot, germs are actually put into your body through the needle. But the germs are either dead or have been changed so that they won't make you sick. Even though these germs can't hurt you, your body still recognizes them as enemies and makes antibody-producing cells against them. Then, if the dangerous form of that germ comes along later, you are ready for it. Your body will make antibodies to fight the germs right away. The antibodies will stop them before they can make you sick.

*Here are the viruses which cause Hong Kong flu. Many people get shots to protect them from the flu.* CENTERS FOR DISEASE CONTROL, ATLANTA, GA

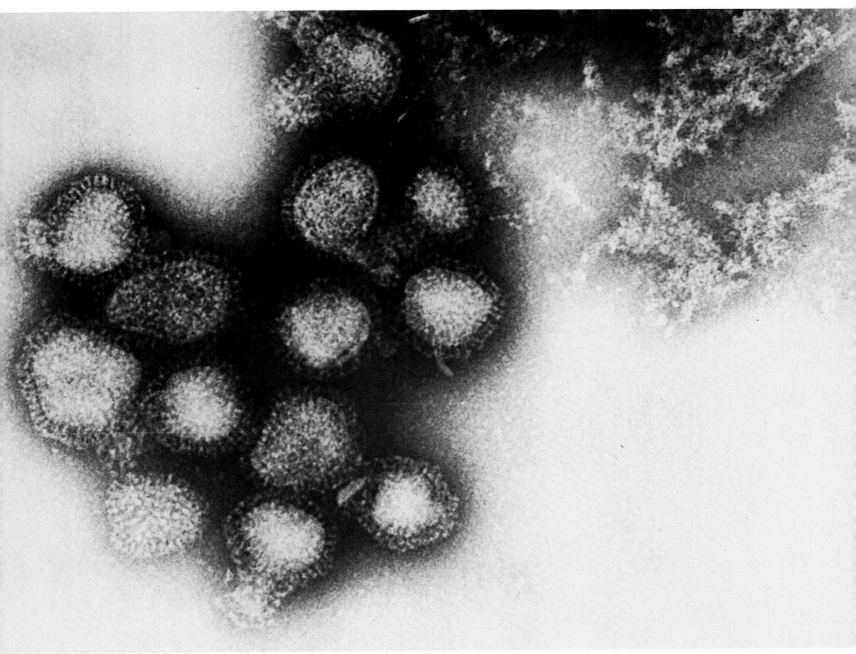

# Antibiotics

Sometimes your body needs help fighting off germs. Some diseases caused by bacteria, such as pneumonia and tuberculosis, can make people very sick or even kill them. Many years ago, these illnesses were the leading cause of death in America. But now we have medicines, called "antibiotics," which can cure these once feared diseases.

*This photo shows how the antibiotic streptomycin keeps bacteria from growing. The stripe in the center is the mold which makes streptomycin. The other blobs are colonies of different bacteria. It takes millions of bacteria to make blobs big enough to see. None of the bacteria can grow near the mold because of the streptomycin it produces. (The top bacteria are* E. coli; *the second causes typhoid; the third one gives people pneumonia; the fourth causes bubonic plague; the fifth can cause many different infections.)* DR. LEON J. LEBEAU, DEPT. OF PATH., U. OF ILL. MED. CENTER

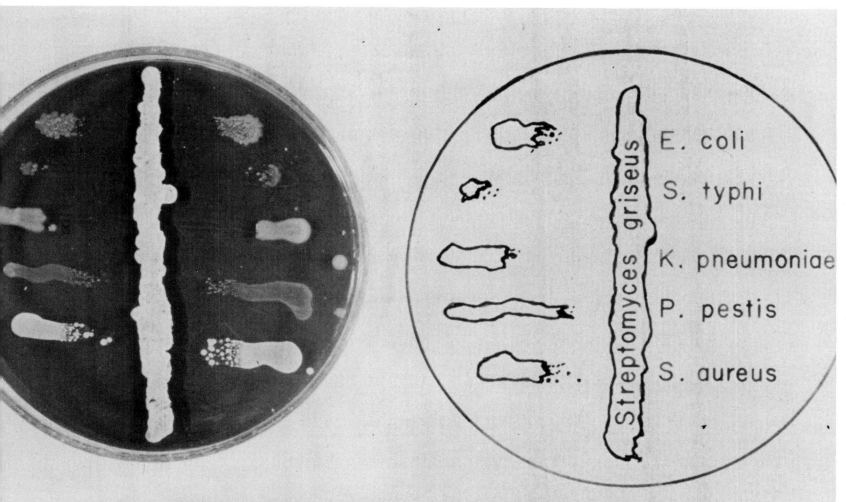

E. coli

S. typhi

K. pneumoniae

P. pestis

S. aureus

Streptomyces griseus

STREPTOMYCIN PRODUCTION

23

The first antibiotic was discovered in 1928 by Doctor Alexander Fleming. He was growing bacteria in the laboratory. By accident, some mold got into one of his cultures. Doctor Fleming noticed that no bacteria grew near the mold. He was smart enough to realize that the mold made something which killed the bacteria or prevented them from growing. He and other scientists studied this material. The first antibiotic, penicillin, resulted.

In the beginning, there was not much penicillin, and it was expensive. It took a lot of mold to make just a small amount of the medicine.

*This is the kind of mold used in the 1940s to make penicillin.* E. R. SQUIBB & SONS, INC.

*Nowadays, penicillin is made by this mold, which makes much more of the medicine than the old kind could.* PFIZER, INC.

With time, ways of making penicillin in larger amounts were developed, and other antibiotics were discovered. Now, there are over eighty different antibiotics. Some are made by molds, like the original penicillin. But others are made in chemical factories. Some antibiotics work best against pneumonia while others fight off tuberculosis. You take one antibiotic for a strep throat and a different one if you have an infected cut. Antibiotics may be given as shots. But more often they are taken as pills or capsules.

*These capsules contain an antibiotic called Terramycin.* PFIZER, INC.

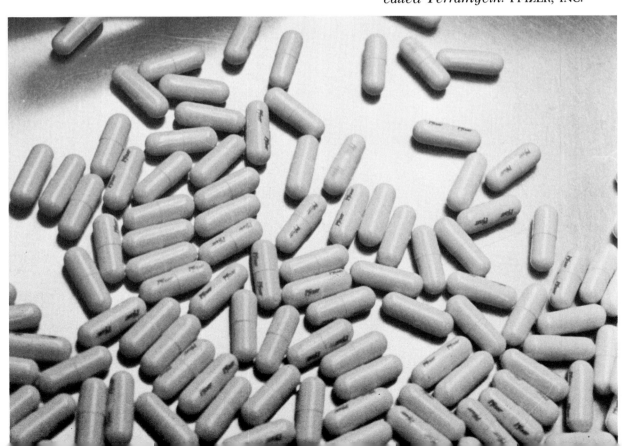

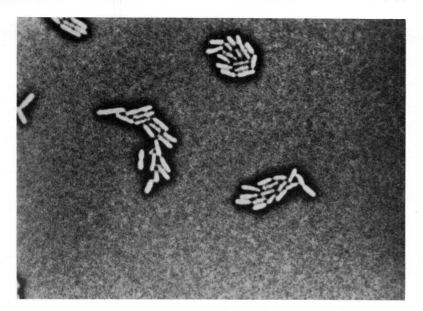 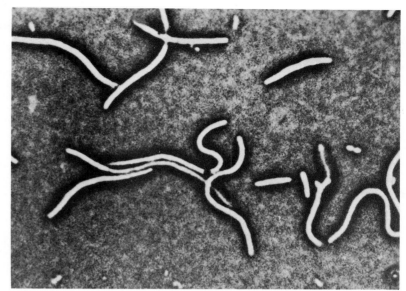

These photos show how the antibiotic Pipracil kills bacteria. The first photo above shows the normal bacteria. In the second photo, Pipracil has made the bacteria become longer and has kept them from dividing. The two photos below show one germ as it becomes weaker, bursts, and dies. PHOTOGRAPHS COURTESY OF LEDERLE LABORATORIES

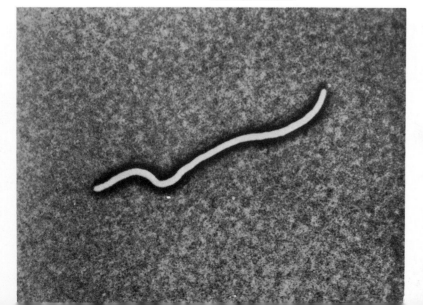 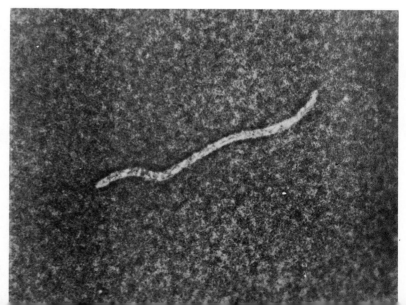

Virus infections are harder to treat than bacterial ones. Luckily, most viruses for which there is no immunization are not very dangerous. Only recently have scientists been able to find medicines which can help cure a few virus diseases. Soon there may be many such medicines.

*Warts are annoying but not dangerous. They are caused by the viruses shown in this picture. (Magnified approximately 150,000 times.)* DR. KWANG S. KIM, NEW YORK UNIVERSITY MEDICAL CENTER

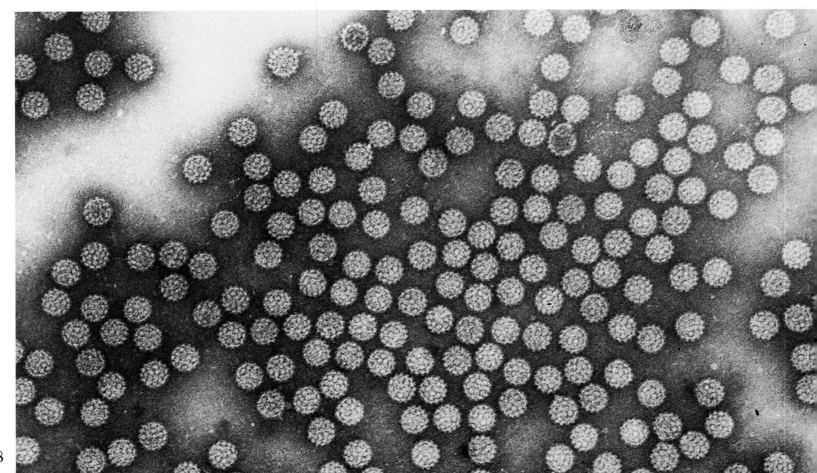

# How Germs Make Us Sick

Some germs live outside the body and cause trouble by making poisons or "toxins." When toxins get into the body, they damage or kill healthy cells. For example, food poisoning is caused by bacteria which can grow in many different foods. Bacteria grow slowly when they are cold. But they can multiply very fast when warm. This is why you should always refrigerate leftovers quickly. If you don't, bacteria can grow on them and make toxins. Then, when you eat the food, the toxins can attack your cells and make you sick.

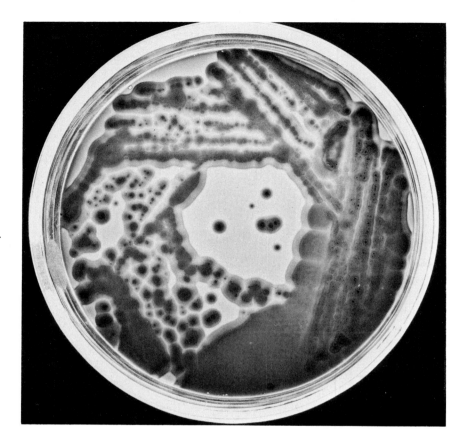

*Scientists often use a small glass or plastic-covered dish called a "petri dish" for growing bacteria. This petri dish shows colonies of the germ which causes botulism.* ARMED FORCES INSTITUTE OF PATHOLOGY

The most poisonous toxin made by bacteria is the botulinus toxin. It causes the deadly disease "botulism." The botulinus bacteria can grow only where there is no oxygen. As they grow, they produce gas. This is why you should never eat food from a can with a bulge in it. It may contain botulinus bacteria. The botulinus toxin is so poisonous that one ounce could kill sixty million people!

Other germs make you sick when they get into your body and make toxins as they grow there. For example, several different germs can cause the stomach and intestinal illnesses which make us feel so sick. Some toxins, such as the one made by common bacteria called "staph" (*Staphylococci*), make people vomit by affecting their nervous systems. Others, like the one which causes the sometimes deadly disease, cholera, make the cells of the intestine lose water very quickly. The water pours into the intestine and then leaves the body too quickly, causing severe diarrhea.

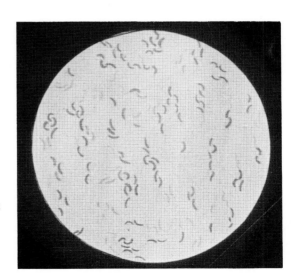

*Here are the germs which cause cholera. They produce a powerful toxin which can make people very sick.* CENTERS FOR DISEASE CONTROL, ATLANTA, GA.

Most bacterial germs grow outside the actual body cells. But tuberculosis germs are different. They grow and multiply inside cells. When they are taken in by the body's macrophages, tuberculosis germs don't die. Instead, they live and grow within the macrophages. Tuberculosis germs need lots of oxygen. That is why this disease usually infects the lungs. When a person with tuberculosis coughs, he releases many bacteria into the air which can infect another person. Less than fifty years ago, tuberculosis was a much feared disease. But now, thanks to antibiotics such as streptomycin, it can be easily controlled.

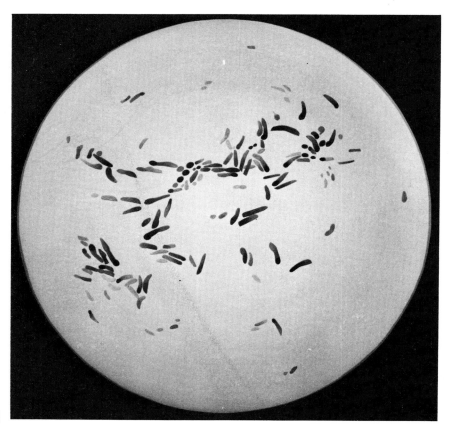

*Tuberculosis germs don't have a regular shape the way most germs do. This photo shows tuberculosis germs seen through a light microscope.* WORLD HEALTH ORGANIZATION PHOTO

*The tuberculosis germs on the facing pa; look quite different through an electr( microscope. These ones have been cut . you can see their insides. (Magnifi( approximately 96,000 times.)* DR. KWANG KIM, NEW YORK UNIVERSITY MEDICAL CENT:

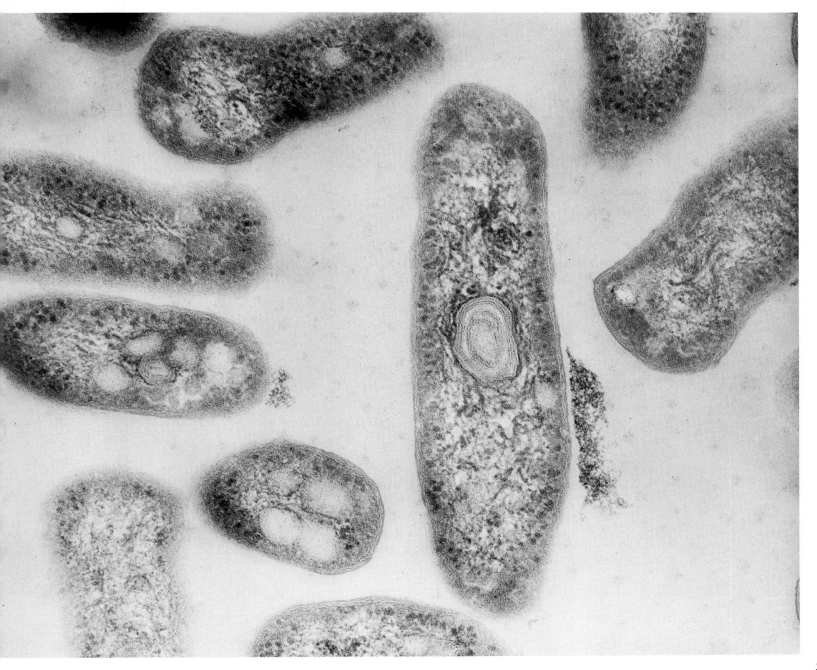

Sickness also occurs when germs enter healthy body cells and kill them. Malaria is caused by germs which live and multiply inside red blood cells. Certain mosquitoes inject the malaria germs into the blood when they bite. Each germ enters a red blood cell. It grows and divides there until the cell contains many malaria germs. All the germs grow at the same speed. The germs burst out of the blood cells at the same time. Chemicals released when the cells break open give the sick person chills and a high fever. Then the germs enter new red blood cells and the fever goes away. Many hours later, when the germs have divided again and burst out, the chills and fever return.

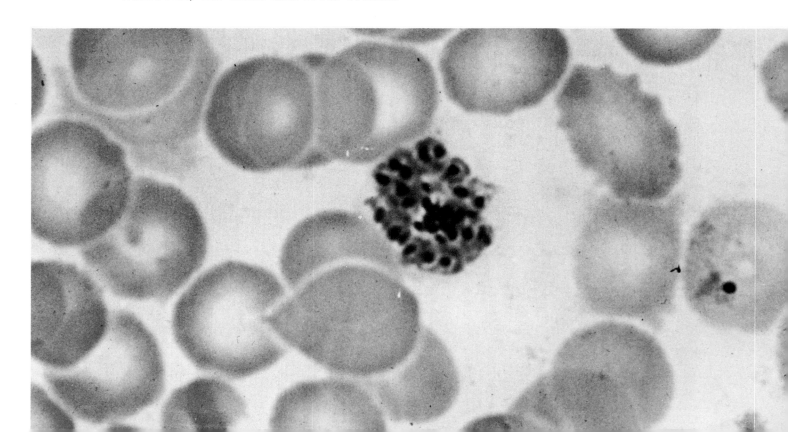

*Whenever you sneeze, thousands of tiny droplets are blown into the air. If you have a cold, the cold viruses will also be blown out and can give someone else a cold.* AMERICAN LUNG ASSOCIATION

Viruses always multiply inside cells. They work by turning our cells into factories for making more viruses. When the cell is packed full of new viruses, it bursts. Then each virus can go on to attack another cell. The stuffiness you feel when you have a head cold results from chemicals released when the virus-infected cells burst. When you sneeze, thousands of viruses escape into the air and can give other people your cold.

*This photo shows human red blood cells. The one in the middle is full of malaria germs about to be released. Each germ will then enter a different red blood cell.* R. IKE ARMSTRONG

# The Future

In America today we don't have to worry much about the most
dangerous germs. With immunizations and medicines, we can
prevent or cure almost every serious disease caused by germs.
People still get sick, however, and a few germs do cause trouble
if they have a chance to grow.

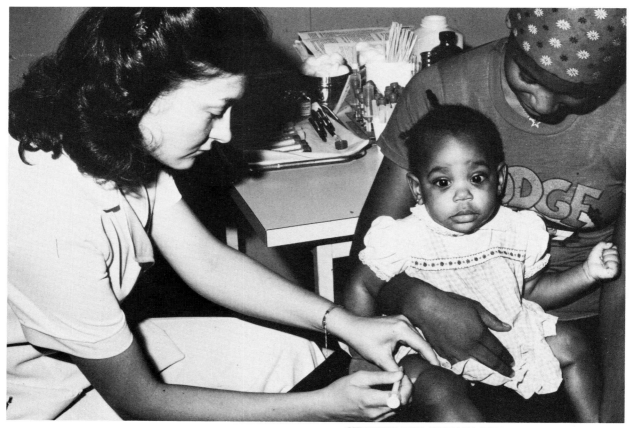

In some parts of the world, germs are more of a problem than they are here. Many countries do not have modern indoor plumbing in all their towns. Diseases such as typhoid and cholera can spread easily through human wastes. So in places without good sewage systems, there can be outbreaks of these diseases. In countries where people are crowded and are not well fed, tuberculosis can still be a problem. When people live close together, germs spread easily. And tuberculosis tends to attack people in poor health. Scientists are working hard to find a surefire way of immunizing against this disease.

We also need better ways to make antibiotics. They are usually quite expensive. This makes them difficult to use in poor countries. Scientists are working on cheaper methods for producing antibiotics.

We need new medicines to treat diseases, too. Doctors hope that they will be able to use some of the body's own defenses, such as interferon, as weapons against disease. With many scientists working on newer and cheaper medicines, the battle against germs should get easier and easier.

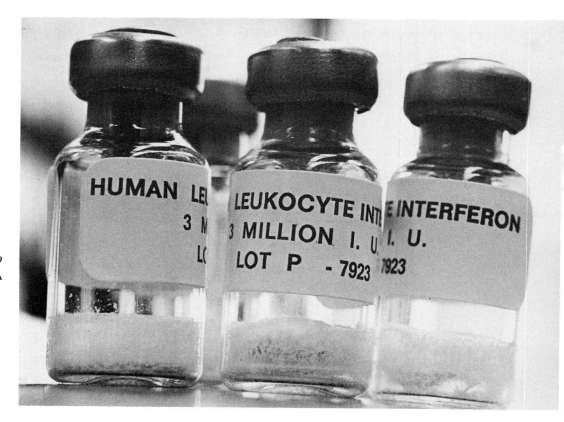

*Interferon is now an expensive medicine, but soon new ways to produce it may make it cheaper to buy.* JOEL FRIED, 1980, FOR COLUMBIA UNIVERSITY COLLEGE OF PHYSICIANS AND SURGEONS

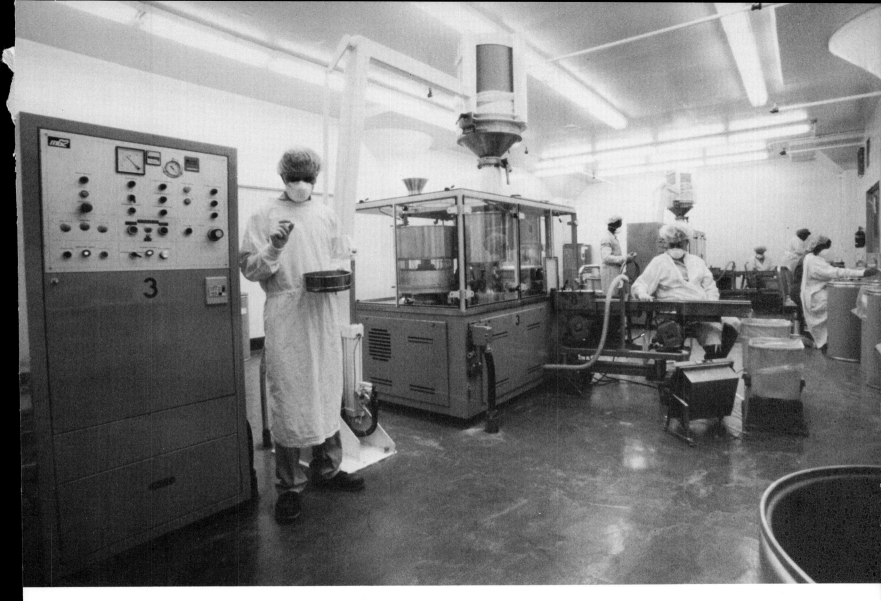

*These machines make capsules of medicines to
help keep people from getting sick. The workers
check the capsules carefully.* PFIZER, INC.

# Index

African sleeping sickness, 10
anthrax, 11
antibiotics, 2, 22-26, 32, 38
antibodies, 15-17, 20
Azactam, 2

bacteria, 3, 8, 11-12, 14, 16-17,
    22-24, 29, 30-32
botulism, 30
bubonic plague, 22

cholera, 31, 37
cold, 9, 17, 35

diphtheria, 8, 18

E. coli, 8, 22

Fleming, Alexander, 24
flu, Hong Kong, 20
food poisoning, 8, 29

immunizing, 18-19, 28, 36, 37

interferon, 15, 38

Koch, Robert, 11

Legionnaire's disease, 14

macrophages, 14, 32
malaria, 10, 34-35
measles, 9, 18
microorganisms, 6-7. See also
    bacteria
microscope, 6; electron, 3, 7, 15, 32
mosquitos, 34
mumps, 18

Pasteur, Louis, 11
penicillin, 24-25
petri dish, 30
Pipracil, 27
pneumonia, 22, 26
polio, 12, 18

rheumatic fever, 17

rubella, 18, 19

scarlet fever, 17
shot, DPT, 18
sneeze, 35
staph (*Staphylococcus*), 8, 31
strep throat, 8, 17, 26
*Streptococcus*, 17
streptomycin, 22, 32

T cells, 15
Terramycin, 26
tetanus, 18
tooth, decay, 3
toxins, 29-31
tuberculosis, 8, 22, 26, 32,
    37
typhoid, 22, 37

viruses, 9, 12, 18, 20, 28, 35

warts, 28
whooping cough, 18